WHALES

Heinemann Library
Chicago, Illinois

Elizabeth Laskey

Designed by Kimberly Saar, Heinemann Library
Illustrations and maps by John Fleck
Photo research by Bill Broyles
Originated by Ambassador Litho Ltd.
Printed by Wing King Tong in Hong Kong

07 06 05 04 03
10 9 8 7 6 5 4 3 2 1

Library of Congress Cataloging-in-Publication Data
Laskey, Elizabeth, 1961-
    Whales / Elizabeth Laskey.
        p. cm. -- (Sea creatures)
Summary: Describes the life of whales, including where they live, what
they eat, what they do, their rate of extinction, and how humans study
them.
Includes bibliographical references (p.   ).
    ISBN 1-40340-960-9 (HC), 1-4034-3567-7 (pbk.)
    1. Whales--Juvenile literature. [1. Whales.] I. Title. II. Series.
    QL737.C4 L26 2003
    599.5--dc21

2002010763

Acknowledgments
The author and publishers are grateful to the following for permission to reproduce copyright material:

Cover photograph by Glenn Oliver/Visuals Unlimited

Title page, icons Brandon D. Cole/Visuals Unlimited; pp. 4, 13, 17B, 23T Flip Nicklin/Minden Pictures; p. 5
David Wrobel/Visuals Unlimited; pp. 6, 26 Todd Pusser/Seapics.com; p. 7 Michel Jozon/Seapics.com; pp. 8,
10, 18 Doug Perrine/Seapics.com; p. 9 Jasmine Rossi/Seapics.com; p. 12 Mitsuaki Iwago/Minden Pictures;
p. 14 James D. Watt/Seapics.com; p. 15 Mike Nolan/Seapics.com; p. 16 Duncan Murrell/Seapics.com; pp. 17T,
28 Doc White/Seapics.com; p. 19 Bob Cranston/Mo Yng Productions/Norbert Wu Photography; p. 20 Bud
Nielsen/Visuals Unlimited; p. 21 Seapics.com; p. 22 William West/AFP/Corbis; p. 23B Robert
Pitman/Seapics.com; p. 24 B & C. Alexander/Seapics.com; p. 25 Ingrid Visser/Seapics.com; p. 27 Daniel
Cox/Oxford Scientific Films; p. 29T Marilyn Kazmers/Seapics.com; p. 29B Phillip Colla/Seapics.com

Special thanks to Dr. Randall E. Kochevar for his help in the preparation of this book.

Every effort has been made to contact copyright holders of any material reproduced
in this book. Any omissions will be rectified in subsequent printings if notice is given
to the publisher.

Some words are shown in bold, **like this.** You can find out what
they mean by looking in the glossary.

Contents

Where Would You Find a Whale?

It is a sunny day in February. You are on a small boat off the coast of Hawaii. For about half an hour now you've been hoping to catch sight of a humpback whale. Suddenly, a fountain of water shoots into the air near you. The gray head of a humpback whale pops up above the surface. The whale keeps rising out of the water until at least half of its body is above the surface. The whale looks like it is as big as a school bus!

The creature then does a half turn and flops back into the water with a loud splash. Just when you think you have seen it all, a tail twice as large as your boat flips up above the water as if to wave goodbye.

Whales, like this right whale, often lift their tails out of the water before making a deep dive below the surface.

What Kind of Creature Is a Whale?

Whales might look like really big fish, but they aren't fish. Whales are **mammals,** just like you.

Whales are sea mammals

All mammals have a few things in common. They are all warm-blooded. This means that their body temperature stays the same, even if the air or water around the mammal is very hot or very cold. All mammals breathe air with lungs. Whales spend time underwater, but they must come to the surface to breathe air.

The beluga whale's body temperature is always much higher than the icy waters in which it lives.

All baby mammals drink milk made by their mothers' bodies. Mammals also have hair or fur. Whales are probably the least hairy mammals, though. Most whales have only a few hairs that disappear before or right after they are born. Right whales, however, keep their hair. They have hairs above and below the mouth that look a little like a mustache and beard.

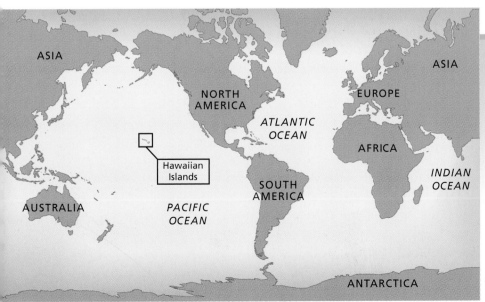

The Hawaiian Islands Humpback Whale National Marine Sanctuary was established in 1997.

How Many Kinds of Whales Are There?

There are about 80 **species** of whales living in the world's oceans. There are two main groups. They are the **baleen** whales and the toothed whales.

Baleen whales

Inside a baleen whale's mouth, you will see wide, flat plates that look like the teeth of a comb hanging from the whale's top jaw. These are baleen. Baleen is made of keratin, the same material found in your fingernails. All baleen whales have baleen instead of teeth.

Baleen whales are the largest animals on the planet. The largest baleen whale is the blue whale. It can be up to 110 feet (33 meters) long. That's about the length of two semi trucks! Other baleens include the bowhead whale, the humpback whale, the gray whale, the fin whale, the minke whale, the sei whale, and the right whales.

This gray whale has white baleen. Blue whales have black baleen, and fin whales have both black and white baleen.

Toothed whales

Toothed whales have real teeth. Some, such as the southern bottlenose whale, have as few as two teeth. The melon-headed whale has 84 to 100 teeth.

Sperm whales only have teeth on their bottom jaw.

Toothed whales are usually smaller than baleen whales. Most are less than 40 feet (12 meters) long. But the sperm whale is very large. It can be 60 feet (18 meters) in length, or about the size of a semi truck. Other toothed whales include the beluga whale, the orca (also known as the killer whale), the pilot whales, all dolphins and porpoises, and the beaked whales.

Beaked Whales

Beaked whales are rarely seen because they live very far from land. They have a jaw that is shaped like a bird's beak. Male beaked whales have only two teeth. Females often don't have any teeth. The two teeth of the strap-toothed whale grow out of the bottom jaw and wrap around the outside of the top jaw.

How Does a Whale's Body Work?

Whales have strong tails and a shape that help them move easily through water. Whales also have a way of breathing that helps them stay underwater for a long time.

The tail is for power

Powerful muscles along a whale's **backbone** move the whale's **tail flukes** up and down. This moves the whale forward. Most whales swim at about 3 to 10 miles (5 to 16 kilometers) per hour. The whale uses its **flippers** for steering and balance. Some whales also have a **dorsal fin** on their back that helps them balance.

A layer of fatty **blubber** and smooth skin covers the whale's bones and muscles. This gives it a sleek shape that helps it swim easily through the water.

The sei whale can go as fast as 40 miles (64 kilometers) per hour, if it needs to escape from danger. The sei whale shown here is a **calf.**

*Each **species** has a different looking spout. The double blowhole of this southern right whale makes a spout shaped like the letter V.*

Blowholes are for breathing

Whales breathe through **blowholes** on top of their heads. The blowholes lead to the lungs. **Baleen** whales have two blowholes. Toothed whales have only one. When a whale is underwater, the blowhole is closed. When a whale comes to the surface to breathe, it opens the blowhole to breathe out.

When a whale breathes out, a fountain of water called a **spout** sprays up into the air. Some people think that water is squirting out of the whale's body. This is wrong. The spray of the spout is a mixture of the air the whale has breathed out and water that was on the surface of the closed blowhole.

Whales can hold their breath a long time

Whales sometimes dive very deep. When they do this, they hold their breath for ten minutes or more. Unlike human swimmers, diving whales do not take a big gulp of air and then hold most of the air in their lungs. Whales do hold some air in their lungs, but they store most of the oxygen they need in their blood and muscles. They use up this stored oxygen very slowly. This is one of the reasons they can stay underwater for a long time.

Sperm whales can hold their breath the longest. Some have been known to hold their breath for more than an hour.

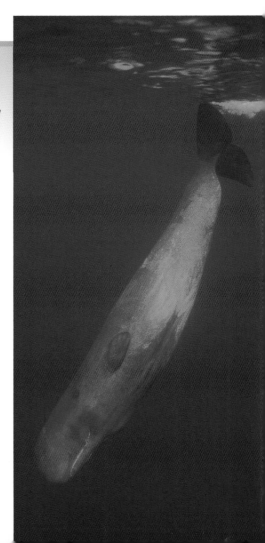

*A sperm whale dives straight down, with its head pointed toward the ocean floor and its **tail flukes** pointed toward the surface.*

? Did you know?

The tongue of a blue whale weighs as much as an elephant.

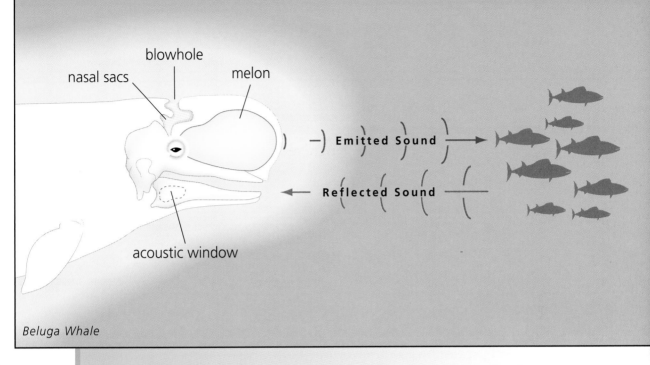

blowhole

nasal sacs

melon

Emitted Sound

Reflected Sound

acoustic window

Beluga Whale

Echolocation helps toothed whales get around in dark or cloudy waters.

Whales don't have all five senses

Most whales do not have much of a sense of smell, and most can't really taste things. But whales do see well both above water and underwater. Whales also have a good sense of touch. The areas around their eyes, mouth, and **blowhole** are as sensitive as human fingers. Whales also have excellent hearing.

Toothed whales are melon-heads!

Toothed whales have a special way of using sound called **echolocation.** To use echolocation, a whale makes clicking sounds. These sounds pass through a part of the head called the **melon** and then move through the water. When the sounds hit an object such as a fish or a rock, an "echo" bounces back to the whale. The way the echo sounds and how long it takes to get back to the whale tells the whale about the object's size and shape and how far away it is.

What Do Whales Eat?

Different **species** of whale eat different food. They also have different ways of hunting for food.

Baleen whales eat small animals

Even though the **baleen** whales are the largest whales, most of them eat very small sea animals called **zooplankton.** One important type of zooplankton is **krill.** Krill look like shrimp and are usually no more than 3 inches (7.5 centimeters) long. Baleen whales also eat small fish.

Baleen whales have different ways of catching food. Right whales and bowheads swim slowly through the water with their mouths open. Zooplankton collect on the baleen and are then scraped off with the tongue and swallowed. Blue whales, fin whales, and minke whales take in one giant mouthful of water. Then they close their mouth and force the water back out through the baleen, which trap the food inside. Humpbacks sometimes swim in a circle, letting air out of their blowholes to form a circle-shaped curtain of bubbles around a group of fish. Then the whales zip through the "bubble net" to scoop up fish.

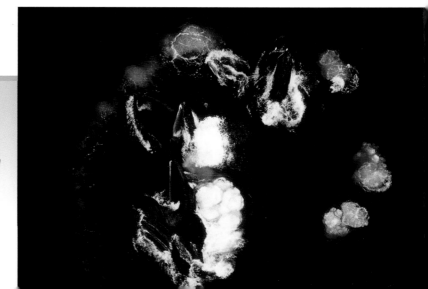

This is what a "bubble net" looks like from above.

Like all toothed whales, this long-finned pilot whale swallows food whole. Teeth are used to catch and hold food, not for chewing.

? Did you know?

Orcas will eat all sorts of things if they can get close enough to it. Scientists have found the remains of a polar bear and a moose in an orca's stomach.

Toothed whales eat larger animals

Toothed whales eat a lot of fish, shrimp, and squid. Some species eat other kinds of food. Orcas may eat seals, sea birds, and even other whales. Orcas hunt in groups.

The favorite **prey** of the sperm whale is squid. Sperm whales even eat giant squid that may be nearly as long as the whale. Giant squid have sharp jaws, eight arms, and two tentacles. No one has ever found a live giant squid. But like their octopus relatives, their saliva may have chemicals that stop their prey from moving. The arms and tentacles have round, sharp-toothed suckers on them. Some sperm whales have scars on their bodies from where a giant squid attacked them with their suckers.

What Do Whales Do?

Whales are famous for lifting parts of their body clear out of the water. Some **species** also **migrate,** or travel, when seasons change. Whales can also **communicate,** or share information, with each other.

Whales breach

When whales lift themselves out of the water head first and then flop back into the water, it is called **breaching.** Usually, a breaching whale lifts about half to two-thirds of its body out of the water. Almost all species breach, but they have different styles. The fin whale lifts about half its body out of the water and then does a bellyflop, which makes a huge splash. The orca sometimes leaps all the way out of the water, twists in mid-air, and lands on its back. Humpback whales may breach more than 100 times in a row.

Scientists think that young whales may breach as a way of playing. Male whales may breach to show other whales how strong they are.

While spyhopping, this southern right whale pumps its tail underwater to keep itself from tipping over.

They look around at the surface

Sometimes a whale will pop its head out of the water so that its eyes are just above the surface. This is known as **spyhopping.** Often the whale will spin slowly in a circle. Scientists think that whales do this to make sure there is no danger nearby.

They slap their flippers and tail flukes

Whales can also make a big splash by slapping a flipper against the surface of the water. This is called **flipper-slapping.** Sometimes a whale will keep its head and most of its body underwater and will raise only its **tail flukes** above the water. Then it will let the tail smash against the surface. This is called **lobtailing.**

Some whales migrate

Many species of **baleen** whale **migrate.** In the spring, they leave the warm waters of the **calving grounds** where they have babies. They travel to the colder waters of their feeding grounds. Some northern right whales, for example, have calving grounds off the coast of Georgia and Florida. They migrate north to their feeding grounds off the coast of Nova Scotia in Canada.

Whales can travel thousands of miles during a **migration.** Gray whales that spend the winter off the coast of Mexico travel 12,000 miles (19,300 kilometers) north to feed near Alaska. The trip takes two to three months. Often hundreds of whales will migrate as a group. Some toothed whales, such as the sperm whale and the pilot whale, also cover long distances while searching for food.

These humpback whales are migrating. Some scientists think the whales may follow patterns on the seafloor.

The beluga whale got the nickname "sea canary" because it twitters and chirps like a bird.

Whales communicate

One way whales **communicate** with each other is by making **vocalizations** such as chirps, moans, grunts, and groans. Scientists are not quite sure how or why whales make these sounds. It may be part of how whales find mates. Male humpback whales will "sing" for up to half an hour when females are near. The males probably want the females to notice them. Whales may also use vocalizations as a warning. Male sperm whales can send out a loud signal to warn another sperm whale miles away of danger.

Do Whales Sleep?

Whales don't really sleep. But they do rest by lying still at the surface. This is called logging. Whales need to be partly awake so they can take a breath from time to time. Often whales will "log" in a group, all facing in the same direction.

These are narwhals in Canada.

What Is Whale Family Life Like?

Many whale **species** form strong family groups called **pods.** The bond between a mother and her baby, or **calf,** is especially strong.

The female gives birth

Whales **mate** about once every two or three years. The female will give birth to a calf about a year later. When a female is ready to have her baby, she moves close to the surface. The calf is born tail first. The first thing the calf does is swim to the surface for a breath of air. Sometimes the mother gives the calf a little help by pusing it upward with her flipper or head.

All newborn whales stick close to their mothers.
This humpback calf hitches a ride on its mother's back.

This pilot whale calf nurses while its mother swims.
Newborn pilot whale calves are about the size and weight of
an adult man.

Babies grow up

Calves of the larger whales can be huge. A newborn
bowhead whale is about 17 feet (5 meters) long and weighs
6 tons. That's about as long as a minivan and about three
times as heavy. To **nurse,** a calf swims underneath its
mother and finds one of the two nipples on her underside.
The calf grabs the nipple in its mouth. A calf nurses about
40 times a day. Calves grow very fast. The largest species
drink so much milk that they gain 5 to 10 pounds (2.25
to 4.5 kilograms) an hour.

Most whales are grown up enough to mate when they are 6
to 12 years old. Whales can live to be about 40 to 50. Blue
whales, sperm whales, and fin whales can live to be 100.

Are Whales Endangered?

Several whale **species** are **endangered.** This means that they are in danger of dying out, or becoming **extinct.** Whales have become endangered because of overhunting in the past. Also, certain human activities have created new problems that put whales in danger.

Whales were hunted in the past

Some **aboriginal people,** such as the Inuit of northern Canada, have hunted whales for hundreds of years. They ate the whale meat and used body parts to make useful items. They hunted only enough whales for their own needs. Starting in the 1600s, Europeans and American colonists began hunting and killing large numbers of **baleen** whales. They hunted whales to make money.

In the late 1800s, whalers began hunting whales with an exploding-harpoon gun. Often, the whale did not die right after being shot. This caused the whale great suffering.

After the exploding harpoon was invented, the number of whales killed each year increased from less than 50 to thousands.

These whalers caught a sperm whale. Later, modern whaling ships were so large that the whales were processed right on the ships.

Whale products were made

The most valuable parts of the whale were its **blubber** and its baleen. The blubber was melted down to make whale oil. In the days before electricity, whale oil was burned in lamps. Later it was used in shampoos, lipstick, ice cream, and many other products. Some of the things made from baleen were umbrella parts, fishing rods, and hairbrushes.

The sperm whale was also worth a lot of money. Its blubber and a waxy material called **spermaceti** from the whale's head made the best whale oil. The spermaceti was used in creams and candles. Sperm whale oil was popular because it burned without causing smoke and it didn't smell bad. Large amounts of sperm whale oil were also used to keep factory machines running smoothly.

Most whale hunting has stopped

By the mid-1900s, most whale products were no longer needed. Electric lights had replaced whale oil lamps. Plastic was used instead of **baleen.** But people worried that some **species** might become **extinct.** Countries then began to make it illegal to kill whales. In 1963, Britain stopped whaling. The United States stopped in 1972, and Australia stopped in 1978.

In 1986, a worldwide **moratorium** made it illegal to kill whales to make money. The moratorium was to last until whales could build up their numbers. Only **aboriginal people** who traditionally hunted whales were allowed to catch a small number of whales. But a few years later, Japan and Norway began hunting minke whales again. Japan said it was doing scientific research. But after the "research" was done, the whale meat was sold. Norway said that whale meat is a traditional food in that country. But most of the meat was sold to other countries. Since 1986, more than 20,000 whales have been killed.

Postcards from 100,000 children around the world who are against whaling were presented to the chairman of the International Whaling Conference at a meeting in Australia in July 2000.

Many beluga whales in the Gulf of St. Lawrence die of cancer. Large amounts of poisonous chemicals have been found in their bodies.

Whales face other dangers

Whales are still in danger because of certain human activities. Oil drilling near **calving grounds** can pollute the water with spilled oil. Chemicals used by farms and factories also wash into the sea. These chemicals poison the sea animals and fish that whales eat. This, in turn, can cause whales to get sick and die.

Whale Strandings

Sometimes one or more whales wash up on a beach. This is called a stranding. Usually, the whales die. In 2000, a group of whales stranded in the Bahamas. Some were bleeding from the ears and eyes. Just before the stranding, U.S. Navy submarines that make loud sounds had been nearby. Scientists think that the sounds were one reason the whales stranded. The submarines now turn off their sound system when whales are near.

Death from nets and ships

Another problem for whales is getting accidentally caught in fishing nets. Thousands of whales die this way each year. A whale tangled in an underwater net cannot get to the surface to breathe, so it dies.

The main cause of death for the very **endangered** northern right whale is getting hit by large ships. Gray whales, blue whales, and humpbacks have also been killed by ships.

Environmental problems

Another possible problem for whales is **global warming.** Some scientists think that global warming has caused ice in the Arctic and Antarctica to melt. This has caused the number of **krill** living at the edge of the ice to fall. In 2001, there were only half as many minke whales feeding near Antarctica as there were in 1991. One reason for this may be that there is not enough krill for the whales to eat.

This type of net has been called a "wall of death" because so many whales and other large sea creatures die in them.

Individuals can help, too. These New Zealanders are working to get stranded pilot whales safely back into deeper water.

Laws help protect whales

Since the **moratorium** went into effect, only a few whale **species** have increased their numbers. Gray whales living along the Pacific coast of North America have increased the most. But only a few hundred northern right whales are left in the Atlantic Ocean. Some scientists fear they will become **extinct.**

The United States has a law against killing or harming any species of whale. Many other countries also have laws like this. Another law gives extra protection to endangered whales in U.S. waters. These whales are the blue whale, the bowhead whale, the fin whale, the humpback whale, the northern right whale, the sei whale, and the sperm whale. Special rules about how fishing nets can be used are part of this extra protection.

How Do We Learn about Whales?

Scientists use modern technology and need a lot of patience to learn about whales.

Scientists take photos of whales

Scientists use airplanes with cameras on the bottom to take photos of groups of whales. The photos show how many whales there are in an area. Scientists collect this **data** for several years in a row. Then they can find out if the number of whales in an area is changing, and they can figure out if efforts to save whales are working.

Scientists also take photos of individual whales. Researchers that study humpback whales take pictures of their **tail flukes.** Markings on the tail flukes help them tell the whales apart. The pictures go into a **catalog** that has data about where and when each whale was seen. When a whale is seen again, new data are added. Scientists have been tracking the movements, behavior, and health of some humpback whales since the 1970s.

The cuts and notches on this humpback whale's flukes make it different from all other humpbacks.

Whale watching is popular because it gives people the chance to see for themselves what amazing creatures whales are.

Scientists track whales over long distances

To study **migration,** scientists attach an electronic tag to a whale's body. Each time the whale comes to the surface, the tag gives off a signal that is picked up by a **satellite** above Earth. The satellite then sends data about where the whale is back to a computer. Scientists can piece together this data to understand where the whales go.

Learning about whales can help save them

The loss of any species can upset the balance of life on Earth. It is hard to know what damage might be done if the largest animals on the planet become **extinct.** The more we understand about whales, the better chance we have of helping make sure these awesome creatures have a future.

☑ The narwhal whale has two teeth. In males, one of the teeth grows into a pointed tusk up to about 6 feet (1.8 meters) long.

☑ Sperm whales can dive 10,000 feet (3,048 meters) below the surface, deeper than any other species of whale.

Male narwhals use the tusks that jut out of their heads as "swords" to fight with each other over a female.

☑ Sperm whales have the largest brain of any animal on Earth. Their brains weigh about 20 pounds (9 kilograms). A human brain weighs about 3 pounds (1.4 kilograms).

☑ The heaviest whale ever was a blue whale that weighed 200 tons (181,800 kilograms). That's about as much as 370 grand pianos weigh!

☑ The blue whale's **spout** is a narrow jet of water that can shoot as high as a two-story building.

☑ The blue whale is the loudest animal on the planet. It can make a sound much louder than the engine of an airplane. The sound can travel hundreds of miles underwater.

The right whale was named by whale hunters. They called it the right whale because it was the "right" whale for them to hunt. It swims slowly and floats when dead, so it was easier for them to catch and kill than other species.

A right whale's mouth is so big a small car could fit into it.

Many tiny creatures live on the bodies of whales. Water fleas dig into a whale's skin and feed on the whale's blood. Whale lice also drink whale blood.

Thousands of whale lice can be found attached to a whale's blowhole, eyelids, and the corners of the mouth.

This blue whale mother and calf are swimming near Baja, Mexico. A blue whale can eat 8 tons (7,300 kilograms) of food a day.

Glossary

aboriginal people first people known to have lived in a particular place

acoustic window fat-filled area in whale's lower jaw that lets in, or receives sound

backbone bone that stretches down the middle of the back

baleen plates that hang down like the teeth of a comb from the upper jaw of baleen whales

blowhole hole in a whale's head that leads to the lungs and is used for breathing. Toothed whales have one blowhole. Baleen whales have two blowholes.

blubber layer of fat under a whale's skin

breaching the lifting of a whale's body out of the water head first. Whales usually lift half to two-thirds of their bodies out of the water and then flop back into the water.

calf baby whale

calving grounds area of the ocean where whales go to mate and give birth. Different species choose different calving grounds.

catalog listing of information and details

communicate share information

data facts and information

dorsal fin triangle-shaped body part on the back of some whales' bodies

echolocation way that toothed whales use sound and echoes to help them find their way

endangered might die out

extinct when a type of animal or plant has completely died out

flipper body part on the side of a whale that helps it balance and steer while it swims

flipper-slapping slapping a flipper against the surface of the ocean

global warming slow increase in the temperature of the Earth. Human activities such as driving cars and heating buildings pump gases into the air that trap heat. Some scientists say this is a major cause of global warming.

krill small, shrimp-like sea creatures with shells that are usually no longer than 3 inches (7.5 centimeters)

lobtailing raising of a whale's tail above the water followed by slapping it against the surface

mate male and female come together to reproduce, or make babies

mammal member of a group of animals that are warm-blooded, have hair or fur, and drink milk made by their mothers

melon rounded mass of fat inside the front of a toothed whale's head

migrate move from one place to another

migration the act of moving from one place to another

moratorium stopping something for a period of time

nurse drink milk from a mother's body

pod group of whales. Often many members of a pod are related to one another.

prey animals that are hunted by other animals for food

satellite object sent into orbit around Earth that can receive information and send it back to Earth

species group of animals that have the same features and can have babies with each other

spermaceti waxy material inside a sperm whale's head

spout spray of water and air that rises above the surface of the ocean when a whale breathes out and is about to come to the surface

spyhopping raising of a whale's head out of the water so that its eyes are just above the surface

stranding when one or more whales washes up on a beach

tail flukes whale's tail

vocalizations sounds made to communicate

zooplankton any of a number of very tiny sea animals that float in the ocean and are eaten by whales and other sea creatures

More Books to Read

Greenaway, Theresa. *The Secret World of Whales.* Austin, Tex.: Raintree/Steck-Vaughn, 2001.

McNulty, Faith. *How Whales Walked into the Sea.* New York: Scholastic Trade, 1999.

Rustad, Martha E.H. *Whales.* Bloomington, Minn.: Pebble Books, 2001.

Index